IT'S TIME TO EAT A WATERMELON

It's Time to Eat a Watermelon

Walter the Educator

SKB

Silent King Books
A WhichHead Entertainment Imprint

It's Time to Eat a Watermelon is a little collectible souvenir book that belongs to the Celebrating Cities Book Series by Walter the Educator. Collect them all and more books at WaltertheEducator.com

USE THE EXTRA SPACE TO TAKE NOTES AND DOCUMENT YOUR MEMORIES

WATERMELON

In the summer sun, so bright and warm,

It's Time to Eat a

Watermelon

Lies a treat that brings us all such charm.

Round and green, with stripes so neat,

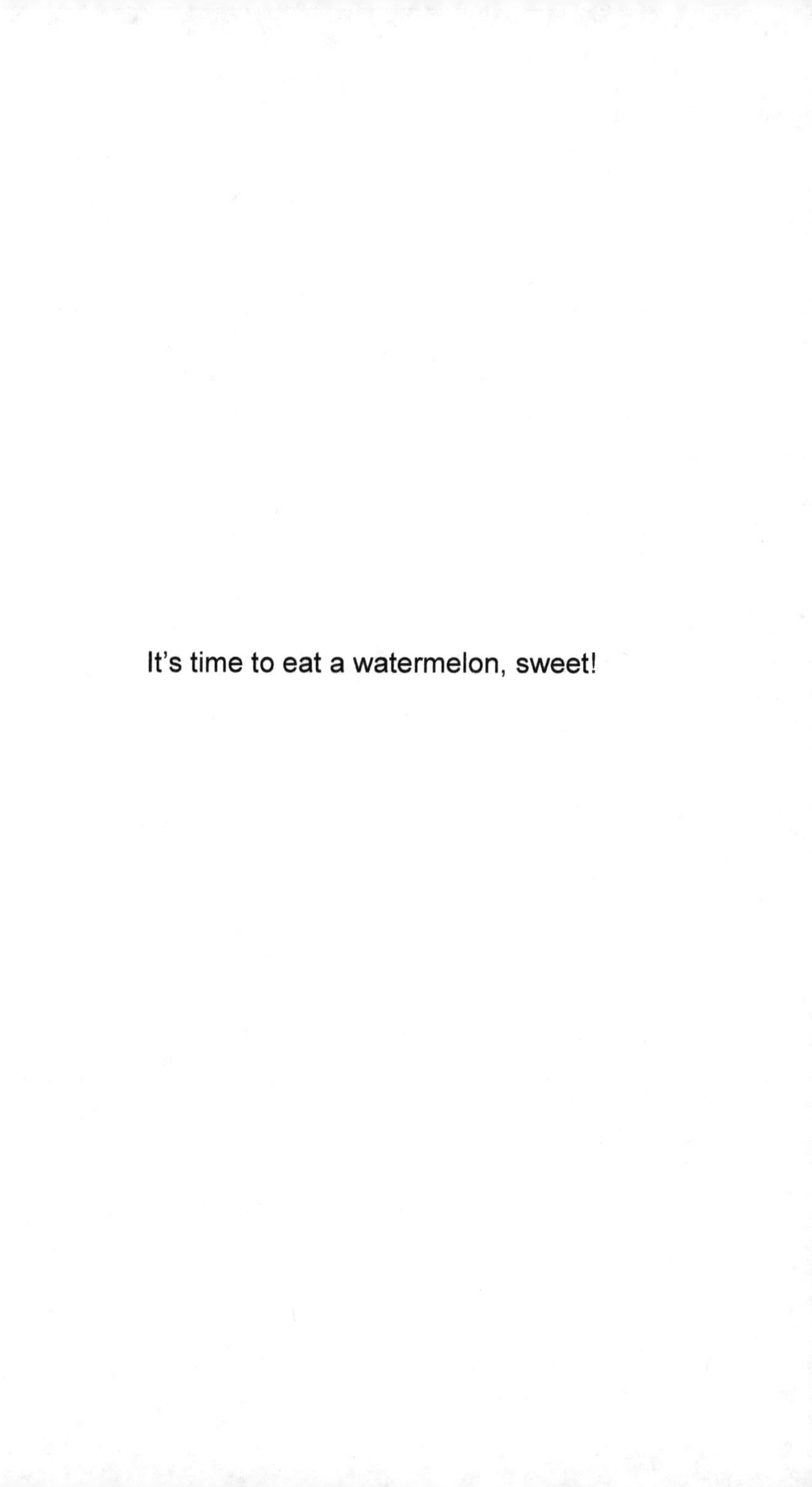

It's time to eat a watermelon, sweet!

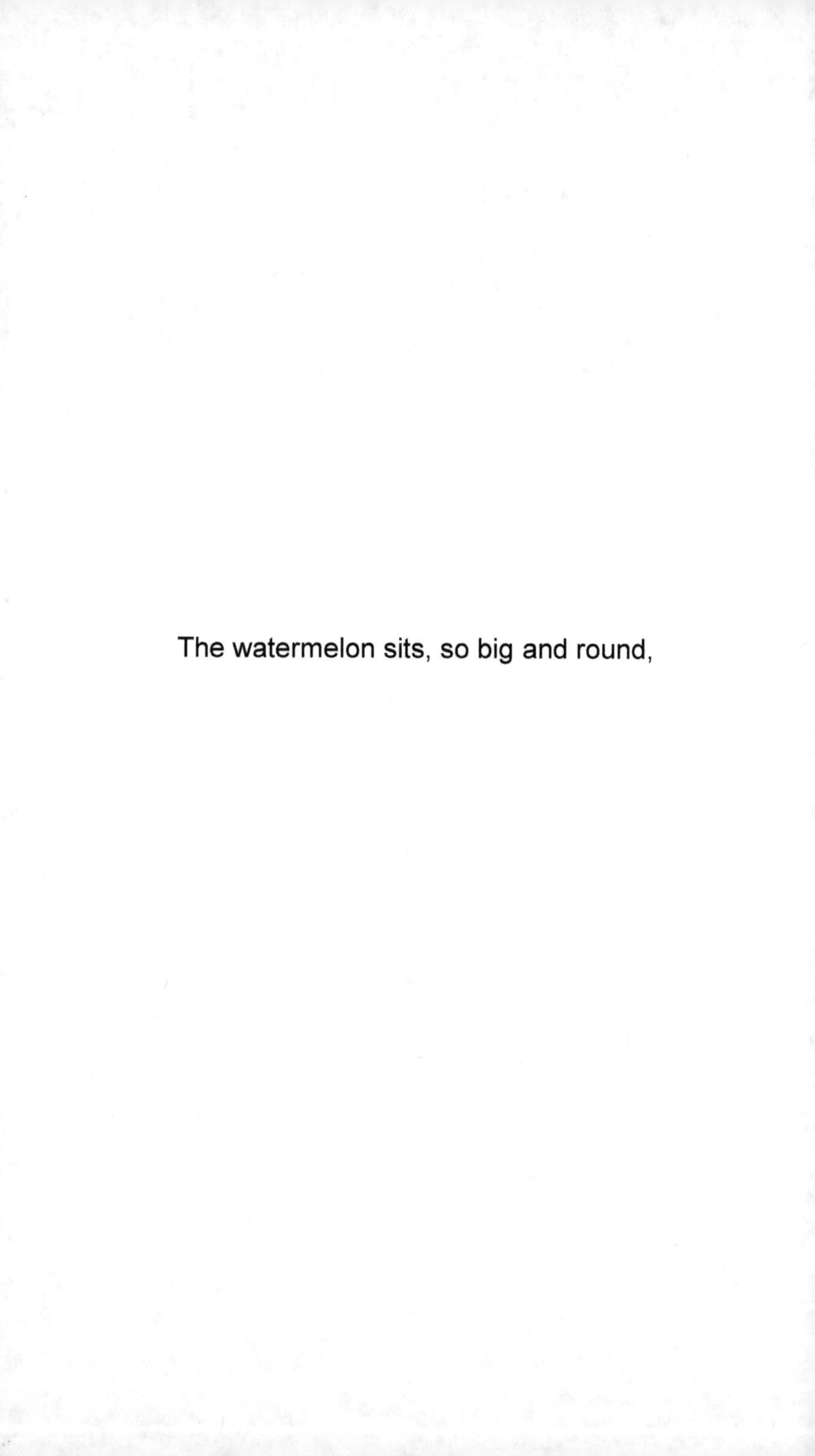

The watermelon sits, so big and round,

Hiding treasures to be found.

With a knife, we cut it through,

A juicy red surprise for me and you!

The juice drips down with every slice,

Oh, doesn't it just taste so nice?

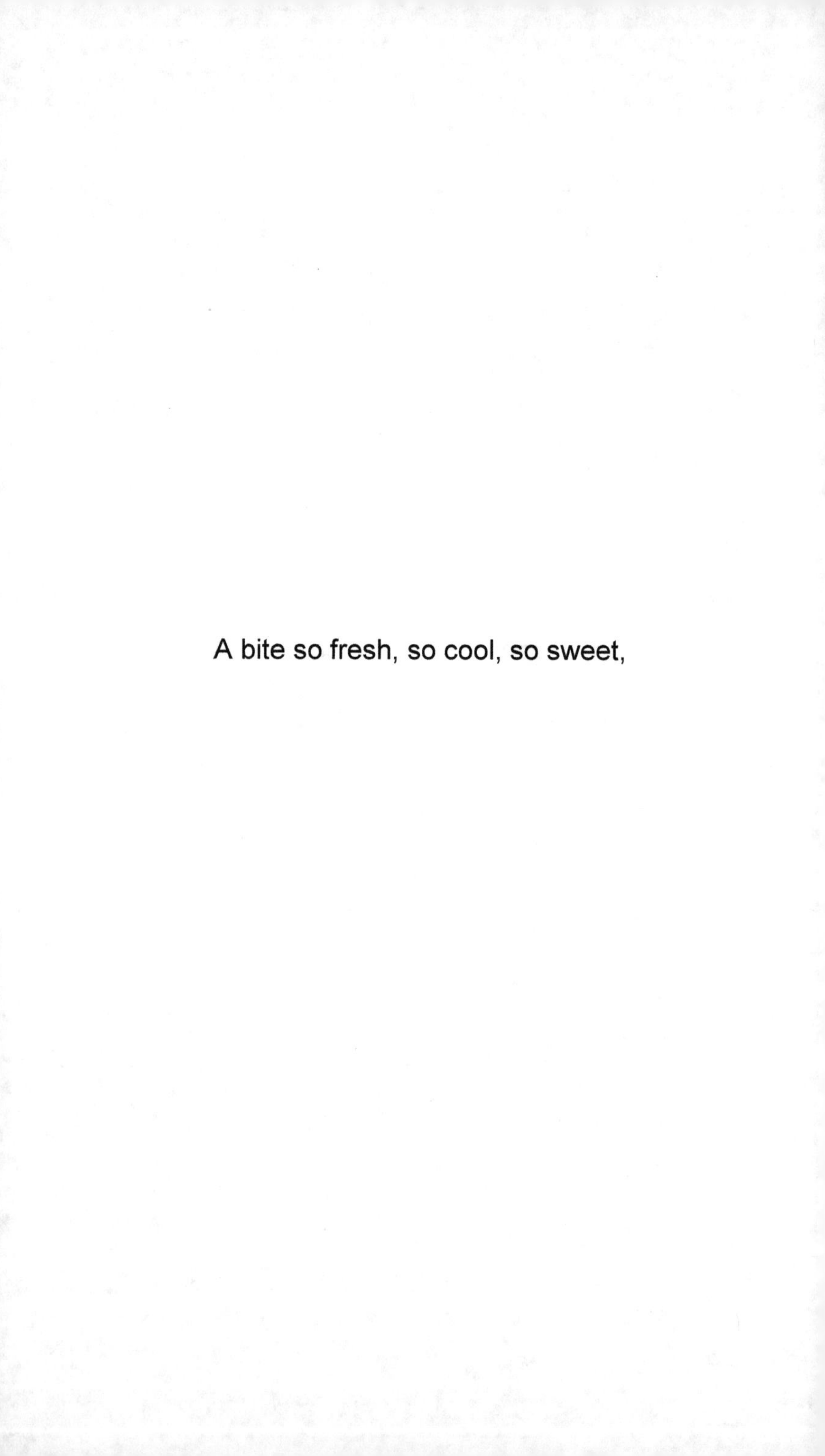

A bite so fresh, so cool, so sweet,

Watermelon's the perfect treat.

Crunchy seeds, black and small,

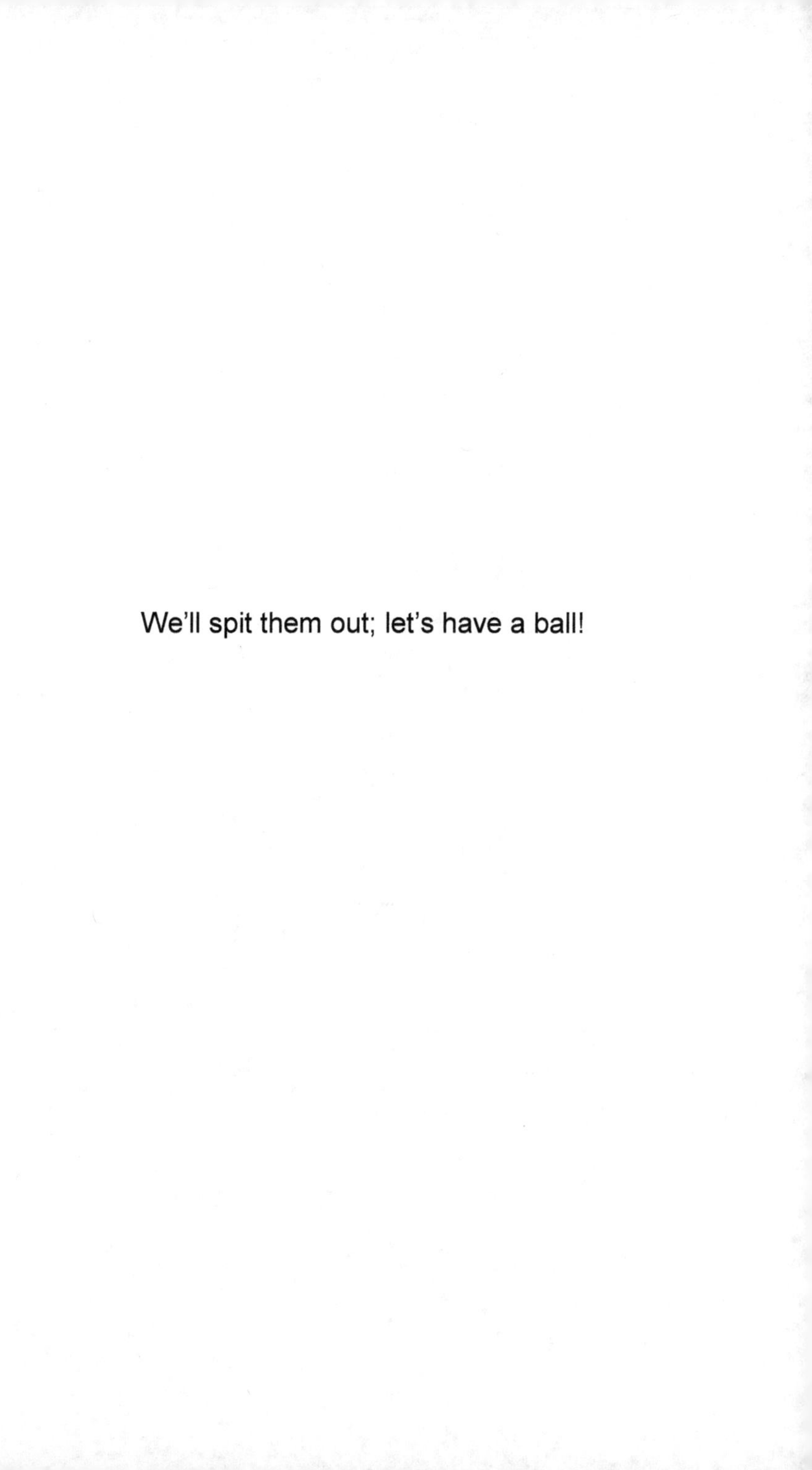

We'll spit them out; let's have a ball!

Each little seed, we flick and fly,

A game of fun under the sky.

It's Time to Eat a

Watermelon

The inside's like a ruby bright,

Sparkling in the golden light.

Every bite, a burst of joy,

For every girl and every boy.

Let's count the seeds, one, two, three,

And see how many there can be!

Or maybe make a seedless wish,

With every slice upon our dish.

The rind is green, the flesh so red,

A happy treat for us to be fed.

We'll eat it up, not waste a bit,

Then pat our tummies as we sit.

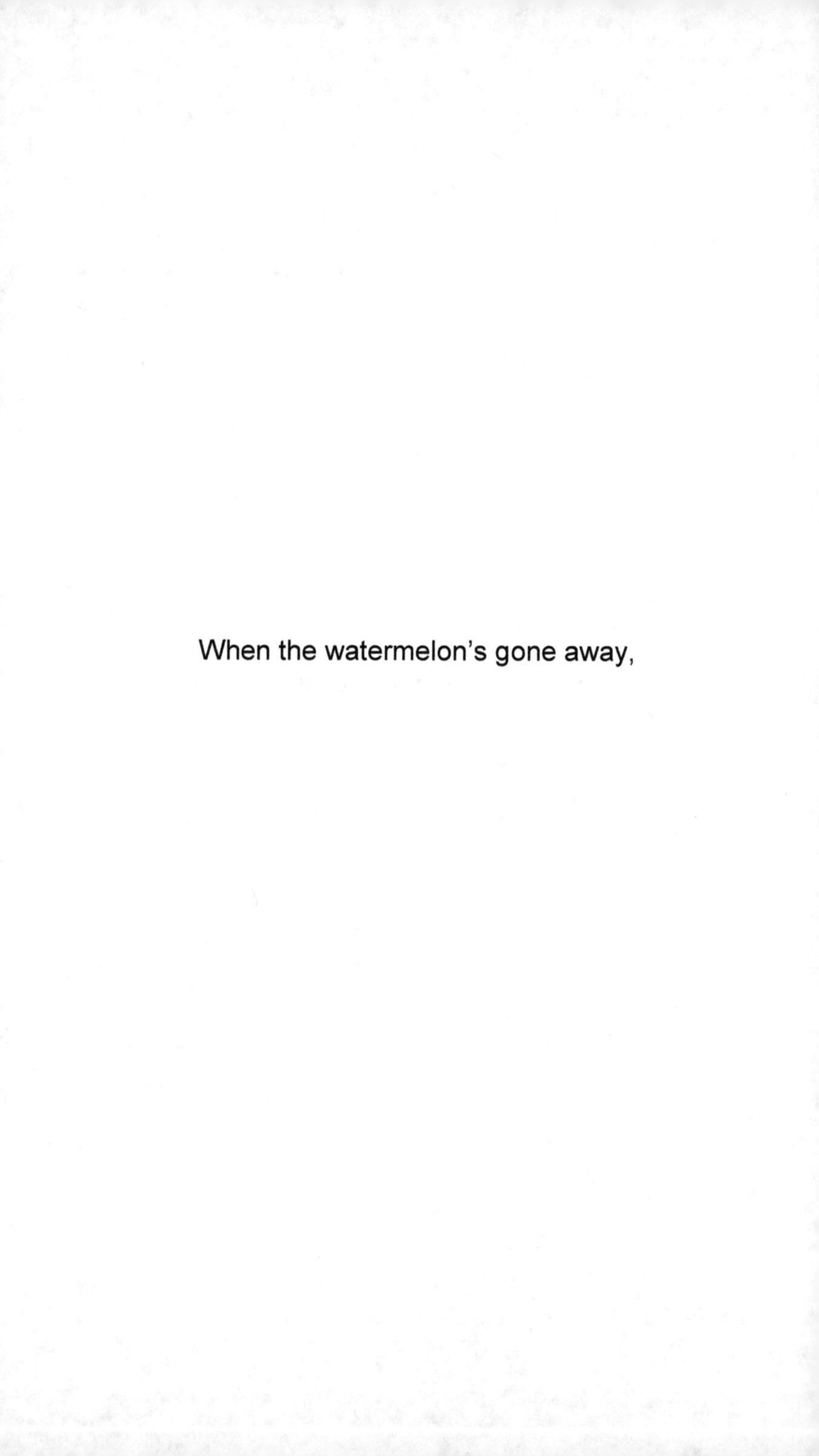

When the watermelon's gone away,

We'll dream of more another day.

But for now, our bellies are full,

It's Time to Eat a

Watermelon

With watermelon, so wonderful.

The sun begins to dip down low,

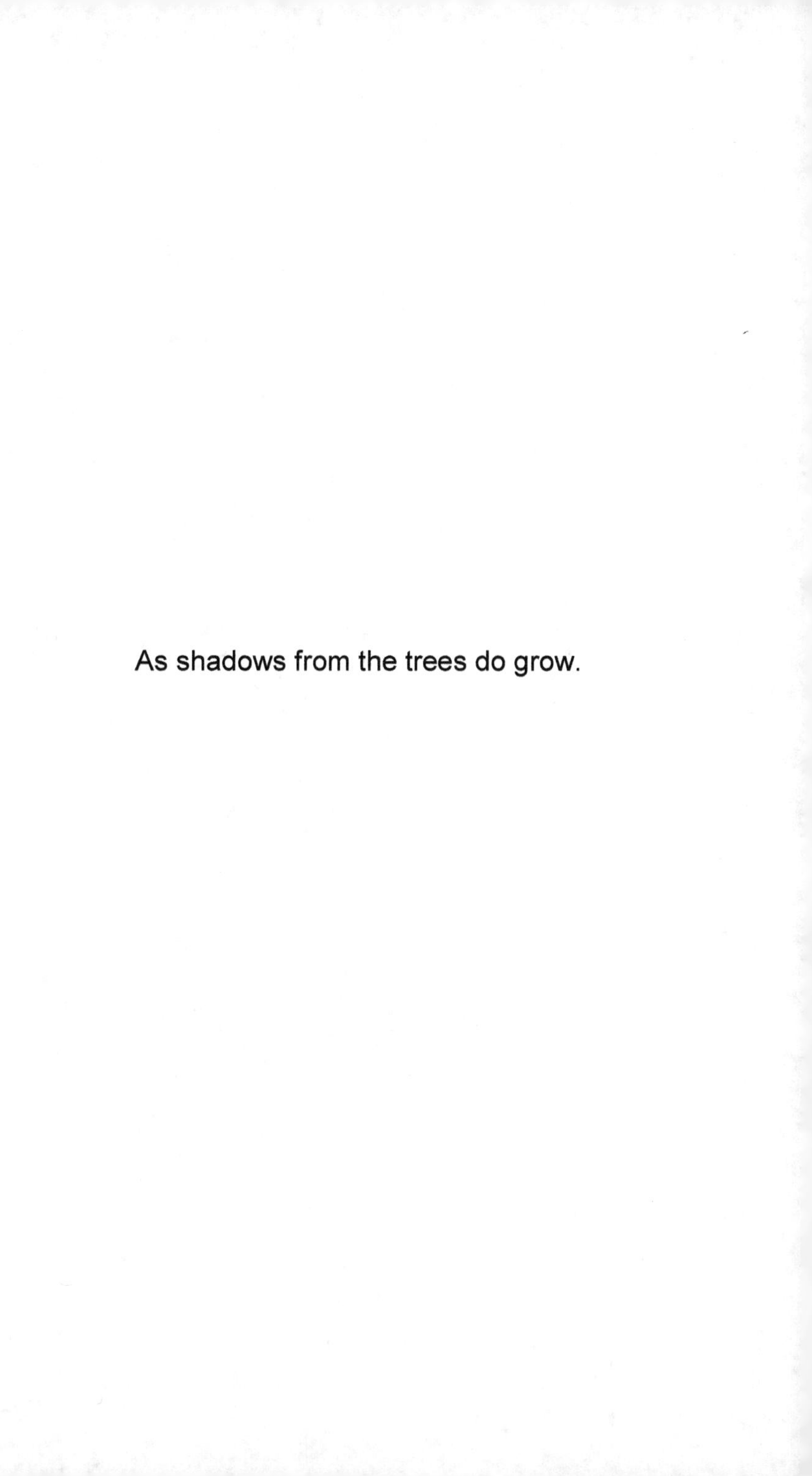

As shadows from the trees do grow.

The day is done, it's almost night,

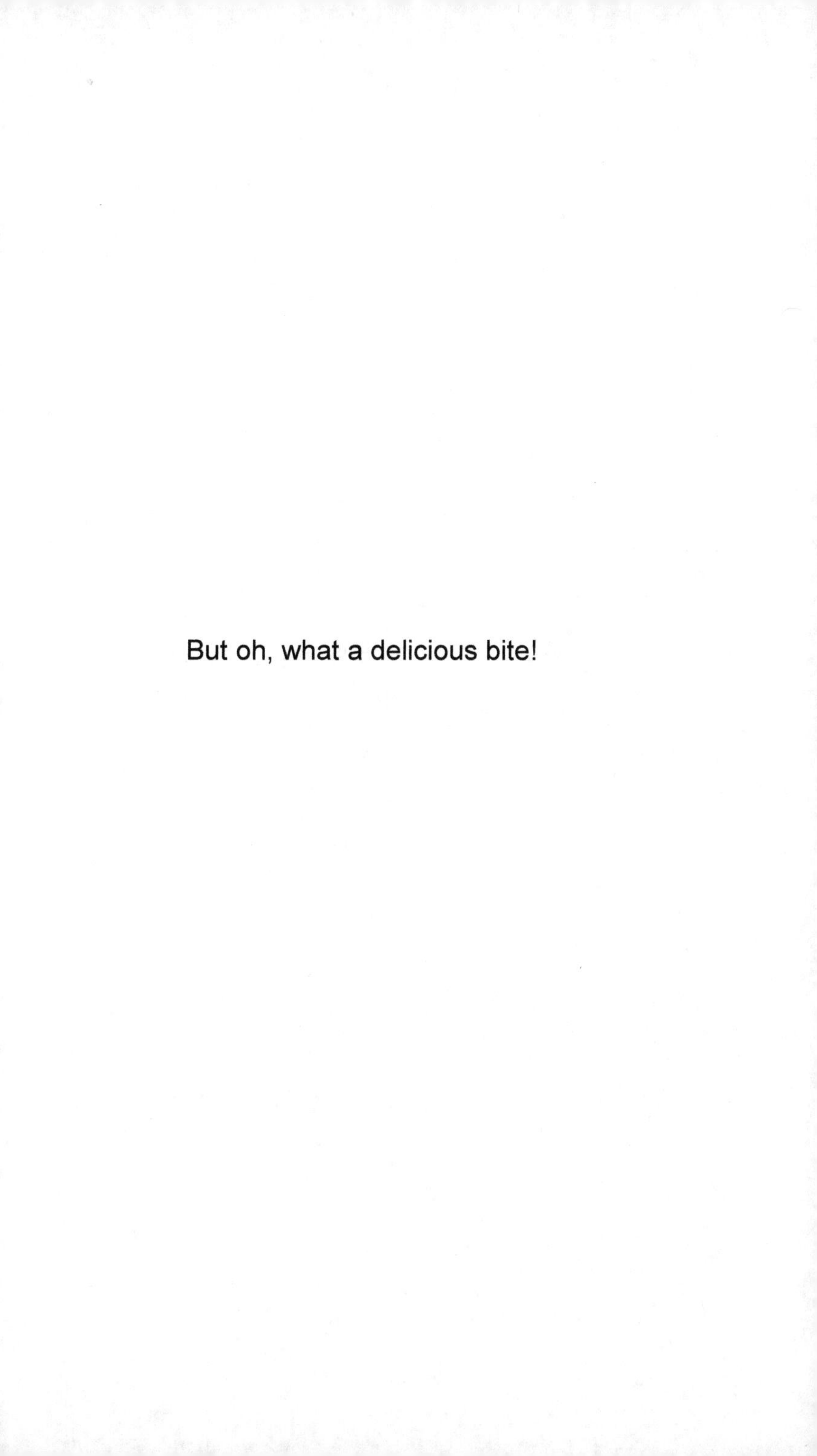
But oh, what a delicious bite!

Watermelon time is always fun,

In the shade or in the sun.

So when the heat is at its peak,

It's Time to Eat a

Watermelon

Remember, it's time for watermelon to eat!

ABOUT THE CREATOR

Walter the Educator is one of the pseudonyms for Walter Anderson. Formally educated in Chemistry, Business, and Education, he is an educator, an author, a diverse entrepreneur, and he is the son of a disabled war veteran. "Walter the Educator" shares his time between educating and creating. He holds interests and owns several creative projects that entertain, enlighten, enhance, and educate, hoping to inspire and motivate you. Follow, find new works, and stay up to date with Walter the Educator™